SensationalSex

AnAdvancedGuideOnHowToReally SatisfyYourPartner

by SuzieHayman

Beautifully Photographed InStunning3D

WantToAddAnExtraDimensionToYourLoveLife?

Simple!JustPutYour3DSpecsOnBeforeYouTurnTheNextPage.

Pages6-93PhotographedEntirelyIn3D

SpecsIncludedOnBackCover

CARLTON BOOKS

Author
SuzieHayman

Photography
JulianNapier

Design
IanFletcher

THIS IS A CARLTON BOOK

© 2002 Elm Grove Books Ltd.
Text copyright © 2002 Suzie Hayman
Created and produced by Elm Grove Books
Limited
This edition published by Carlton Books Ltd. 2002
20 Mortimer Street London W1T 3JW

All rights reserved. A CIP catalogue record for
this book is available from the British Library.
ISBN 1 84222 742 4.
Printed and bound in Hong Kong

The authors and publisher have made every
effort to ensure that all information is correct
and up to date at the time of publication.
Neither the authors nor the publisher can
accept responsibility for any accident, injury or
damage that results from using the ideas, information or advice offered in this book.

The publishers would like to thank the following for
the loan of their products www.passion8.com and
www.sh-womenstore.com

Contents

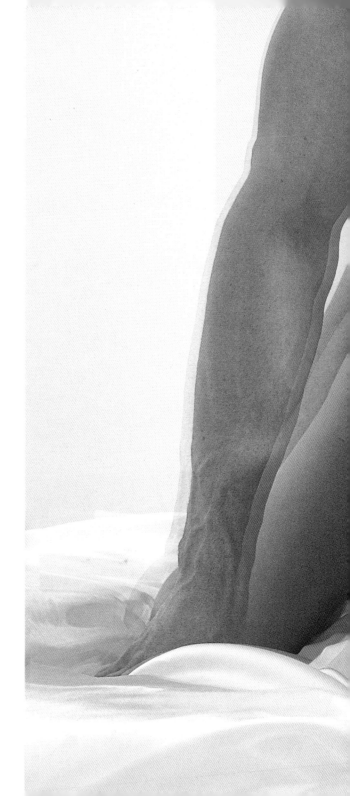

Sex can be more than fun, it can be sensational. It can thrill and electrify; add an extra dimension to a relationship and change the way you see yourselves.

In my opinion, and experience, as a counsellor, the best sex is in a loving, and committed relationship. But love is also enhanced when accompanied by a vibrant, active and evolving sex life. We enjoy the sensations of sex and the way we share these sensations creates and confirms a bond with the person we love.

Today, effective forms of birth control mean we make love for pleasure far more often than we do for procreation. Our longer life expectancy and health provides us with more years to enjoy sex, and to enjoy it with the same partner. In the twenty-first century we have great expectations of sexual pleasure, and of successful relationships which include sex for all our lives. Successful sex is about knowing yourself, knowing how to give and receive pleasure, with self-assurance, self-esteem and self-worth.

To sustain a relationship and to make our love lives a continuing pleasure, it helps if we focus on what we do, and how and why we do it. Love-making is not an instinct we are born with but a skill we learn. There should be no embarrassment in recognising that most of us could learn new skills and techniques. Every now and then we could benefit from considering how well we communicate with our partner. This book will help you do just this. It's an advanced course in what goes on between men and women.

In order to enjoy and expand your sex life, see how other couples approach the issues. Look at the way other people make love, think about it, talk about it, show each other how to try something new. This could help you overcome your inhibitions, increase your confidence and successfully communicate your feelings and desires to your partner. Successful sex is about knowing yourself, knowing how to give and receive pleasure.

1. expectations

Sex, according to some experts, is 90 percent fantasy and 10 percent friction. In other words, what goes on in your head has more effect than what you do with or to your body. Caring about your partner's feelings and sensations, and believing in yourself as a lover matters more than your performance. This also works when you have physical problems that hold you back. The disadvantages occur if your beliefs or expectations about sex are wide of the mark. However good you may seem at sex, you and your partner may be missing out.

There are a number of common myths that many people assume are true about sex. Some are amusing, some are silly, but many are harmful and unhelpful. One is that men and women are different, in what they want and what turns them on. Men, according to this myth, are "only after one thing" - SEX. Women enjoy sex ONLY when it comes with romance and a wedding ring. In my experience, there are many more similarities than there are differences between what men and women desire, experience and enjoy. Men do want romance and the security of a long term, one-to-one relationship. They enjoy their love lives better within the boundaries of a committed relationship. Women do experience lust, desire and raunchy, red-hot sensation. They also enjoy romance, steady relationships and commitment from their partner.

Equally confused are myths about sexual instinct. Many people assume that part of growing up is knowing about sex. In fact, making love is a skill you learn, not an instinct you are born knowing how to use. You need to discover what turns you on and share your discoveries with your partner.

A myth, which many people still believe, is that masturbation is bad for you. Children often explore their bodies, but parents, thinking they are doing the right thing, may tell them off. It doesn't stop the exploration but does leave you feeling guilty and bad. Masturbation is normal and natural at all stages in life. It's beneficial and enables you to learn your own responses and enjoy yourself.

To assume that men and women have very different attitudes and goals can stop you communicating with the opposite sex. After all, if you really believe that men and women come from different planets, what is the point in trying to find common ground ? You are a different species - communication is impossible!

If you unthinkingly accept that sex is instinctive, you won't make the effort to learn or improve. If you uncertain about sex, you think there is something wrong with you. A man who has "off days" and a woman who would like to "make the running" in her relationship both feel as if they are behaving abnormally or embarrassing their partner. Couples who like to spice up their sex lives with the odd daydream or erotic game worry uncomfortably that it means something is wrong with themselves or their relationship.

The problem with these myths is that they tend to prevent you learning how to please yourself and how to please your lover. They make you feel guilty, incompetent, foolish and wrong. Paul and Steffi, for instance, came to counselling because they were having problems in their relationship. Their main concern was the increasing rows and disagreements between them. What soon emerged was that sex was an area each felt uncomfortable discussing with each other. They both felt disappointed in their sex life and that it wasn't nearly as good as they expected or wanted it to be. Steffi felt Paul should know how to please her, but she was extremely reluctant to tell him or show him how she liked to be touched in case he was shocked or disgusted to learn she masturbated. Paul was in a spin about confessing he did not always want sex and would have preferred to kiss and hug and whisper his sexual fantasies. When they had the chance to talk about their confused sexual relationship it removed the strife and they became happy, thoughtful, satisfied lovers. Finding out that they were not at all unusual or unacceptable made Paul and Steffi realise that communication was an important sexual skill they'd not considered before.

The final myths of sexual difference are that men are always ready for sex and an erect penis is all a woman needs for satisfaction. Men have moments when they would prefer a cuddle, and penetrative sex does not always hit the spot for a woman. Taking time, talking, stroking or kissing often provides a deeper sense of satisfaction for couples who at other times enjoy a passionate and athletic relationship.

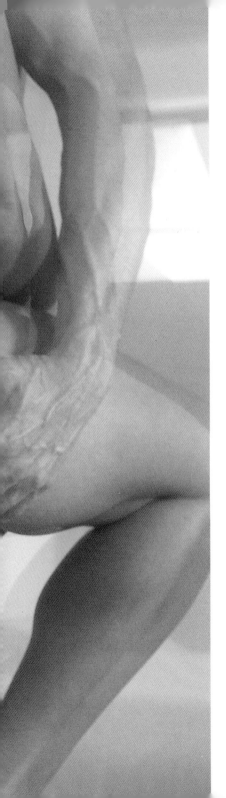

We all learn about love, relationships and sex from the things we see and hear all around us. Naturally, our important first role models are our family. As we grow up the way parents or carers talk about sex, refer to sex or ban all mention of sex tells us plenty. Your upbringing can leave you knowing your curiosity is both justified and worthy of being satisfied, and with the confidence to ask questions of those you trust. It can result in high self-esteem that enables you to approach loving relationships with assurance.

Alternatively, it may leave you feeling guilty, tongue-tied, embarrassed or down-right afraid when it comes to sex or your interest in it, with a lack of self-worth that causes problems. From an early age children often explore their bodies but parents may slap small hands and tell the child to stop being dirty. Parents always want to do the best for their children but instead of helping and protecting them, as parents hope, this may leave them with a a legacy of shame and embarrassment and is a poor lesson.

Most people find themselves somewhere in-between a happy, confident approach to sex and a tongue-tied, guilty, embarrassed attitude. Friends, partners, failures and successes can make all of us waiver from relaxed to embarrassed. I have normally found that at some time most people need reassurance that what they want and enjoy in a relationship is achievable and acceptable. Enjoying sexual fantasies does not indicate that your sex life is in trouble. It is much more probable that you are enjoying a rip-roaring sex life. Couples who have a healthy fantasy life have been found to be in relationships in which they describe themselves as being good fun in bed and happy out of it.

How to please yourself and how to please a partner are all skills we learn. The learning never stops because we all change and develop as time goes on, and picking up and perfecting these skills can be a lot of fun. Sensational sex is something you have when you and your partner can feel comfortable in making suggestions, trying out things and making your sex life exactly what the two of you want it to be. This may be a case of enjoying loving sex in a way you have found is right for you: no surprises and no disappointments. At certain times in your life it may be that you do something new just about every week. It is up to you, but you will never know what suits you both unless you ask so the other vital skill is learning to talk to each other about sex.

BeliefsExpectations&Myths

Do's&Don'ts

Before we are fully aware of our own sexuality we start to learn about sex by listening and watching. We see it on television and in films, usually elevated and enhanced beyond normal everyday reality. All sorts of products are sold to us underpinned by the message that using them will make us more desirable and sexy. Perhaps sex has been discussed in the family. It will certainly be discussed, at length, between friends. At school, sex education may cover contraception but often skips the emotional and physical nature of sex. To find out about the practicalities involved in sex however, we usually learn by experimentation and discovery.

As a baby or a toddler, you probably explored your own body to find out where you began and ended, what feels good and what feels better. You may well have had your hands slapped and been told off. This may have given you the impression that your body was dirty, your thoughts and feelings perverted, and that sexual exploration was a thoroughly bad and unacceptable behaviour. Boys masturbate but often do so hurriedly and furtively in order not to be caught which, naturally, gives them an excellent grounding in premature ejaculation. Girls may masturbate, but have learned that it is unwise to tell their parents or friends and consequently their future partners. It is not surprising that as adults so many of us find it hard to appreciate, love or pleasure ourselves and find it just as hard to allow or show a partner how to do so.

Self-exploration and self-understanding are vital to good lovemaking in a relationship. A sad result of being made to feel that any sensual exploration is bad is that it not only tells you that your sexual desires are unacceptable, but that you are too. If you have been brought up to think that you should not touch yourself you may feel that not only are your desires wrong but you believe your body must also be wrong. Doctors, counsellors and agony aunts often hear from people convinced that their bodies are too fat, too thin, too tall, too short. Many of us are sure our genitals are the wrong shape, the wrong size, the wrong colour or texture; that they smell, are far too hairy or not hairy enough. In every case, what you have is a perfectly normal, perfectly acceptable body. So the first step in having sensational sex is to learn to love your own body. The truth is, it is harder to love someone if you do not love yourself. It is even harder to enjoy sex.

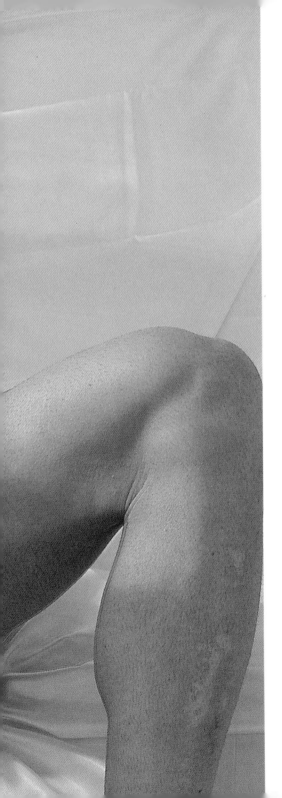

It isn't easy enjoying sex or pleasing a partner until you can satisfy your-self. There are several advantages to being an expert in the art of self-satisfaction. One is that it enables you to understand exactly which touches and caresses, on particular parts of your body, are capable of driving you wild. Of course, almost every man responds to having his penis stroked and most women to having their nipples stimulated. Some people like firm touches, some gentler, some find caressing the genitals and breasts is essential to their sexual arousal but others favour a different part of their body. One person might be brought to instant climax by having a toe sucked or the back of the neck stroked. You do not know unless you have tried. You can't help your partner please you unless you are prepared to tell them what works for you, ask them what stimulates them and be prepared to listen.

You can begin to wake up your sex life by appreciating yourself. Strip off, stand in front of a mirror and look at yourself. Imagine what someone who loved you would see. A loving partner does not start by seeing you in bits – good or bad. A partner sees a complete person. Try and look at yourself as though there is nothing to improve and try believing that there is nothing to improve. You are desirable whatever your shape or size, and you need to admit it.

Learning To Please

Next, close your eyes. Slowly and carefully run your hands all over your body, gently feeling and experiencing yourself. Notice the different textures of your skin. The skin on your face is different to the skin on the back of your hands, the soles of your feet or the inside of your thighs. Your fingertips are your sensors, but experiment using the palms of your hands. There maybe parts of your body that respond better to being smoothed by an open hand than caressed with the fingertips. Open your eyes and do this again and watch each part of your body as you touch and explore it. Some actions may make you shiver, others may produce goose-bumps and some may make you want to close your eyes and purr. We may not know how to give ourselves pleasure until we have explored and discovered our own buzz factors, and neither will our partner.

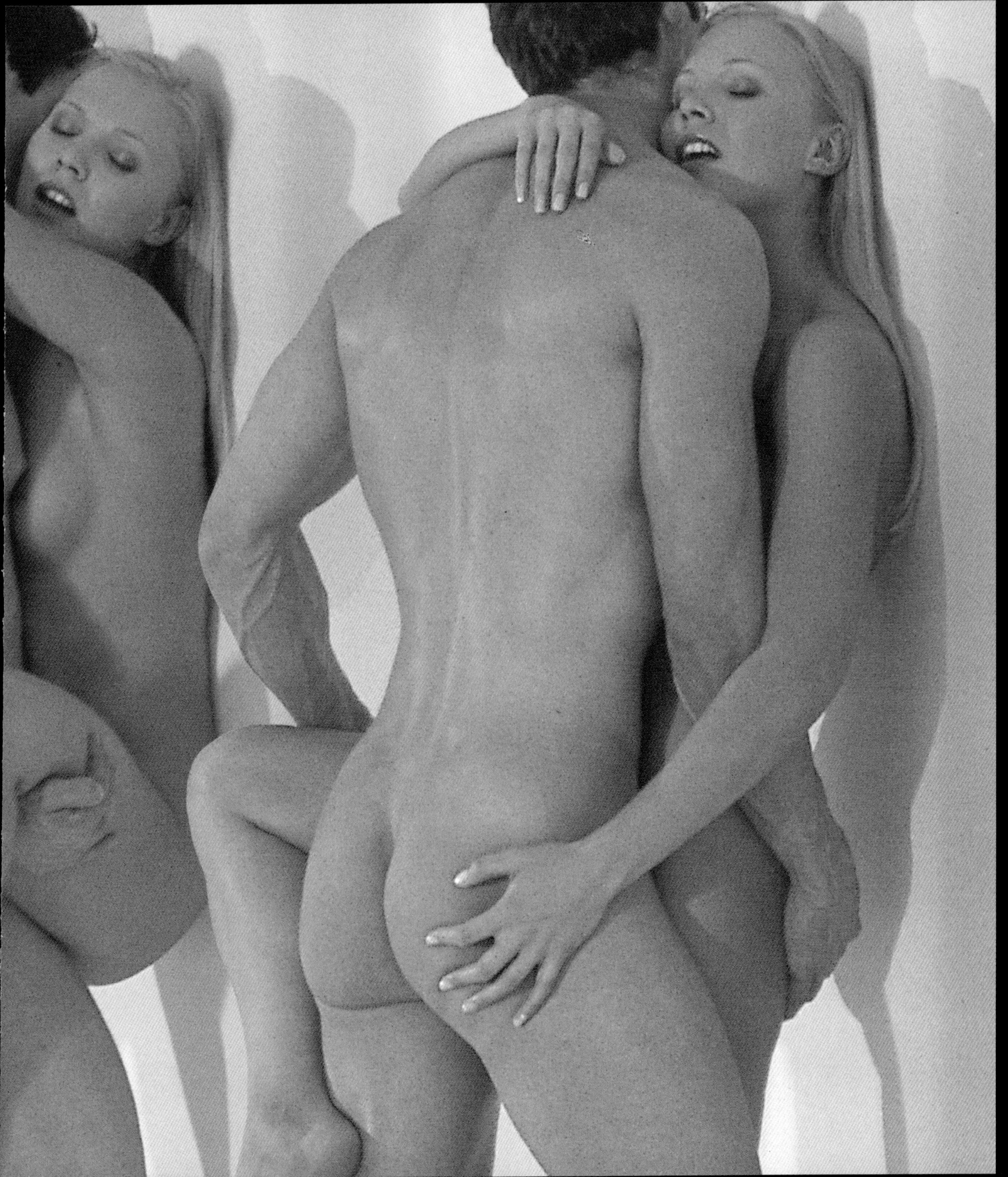

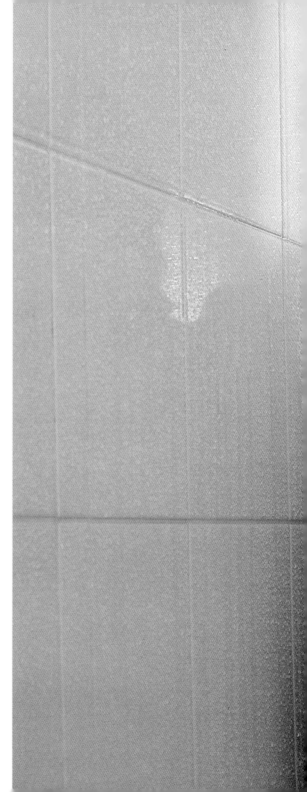

How we learn

Make a special time when you can be warm and comfortable and private. You might like to sit or lie down and you can do this in the bath or shower. Again, run your hands slowly over yourself from top to bottom, side to side and all around. Concentrate on what seems especially pleasant. You may be surprised at what simply feels good. Everyone loves and responds to the power of touch. There is nothing quite as comforting and valuing as being stroked. Stroke a cat gently and repetitively and it will purr. Try it on yourself and you will soon see why a cat purrs! Allow your mind to relax and enjoy the sensations and you will find that every bit of your body reacts to being touched.

Once you have found what makes you purr by stroking yourself, you can concentrate on finding the next level: the level beyond the pleasant tingle to sexual arousal. For women, there are obvious places to touch: your nipples, your entire breasts, your labia and your clitoris. Most of your face and neck are sensitive – lips, earlobes, under your jaw are worth exploring. You may find sucking, and nibbling on fingers gives you as much pleasure as stroking your toes. Many people notice the inside of their elbows and thighs and the backs of their knees are extremely sensitive. You may find your buttocks or the small of your back, around your anus, and down the inside of your thighs are also very receptive areas. Stroke and tickle and experiment with different levels of touching to see the effect they have on you. You can brush lightly with the tips of your fingers, stroke with your whole hand, or scratch gently with your nails. You can dabble with your fingertips, rub lightly or more firmly. You can use the heels of your hands to massage rhythmically or press and knead with your thumbs. If you are in a bath or shower, use the flow of water from tap (faucet) or shower head to stimulate yourself. Experiment with the various caresses that can really arouse you and bring you to climax. The vast majority of women are capable of more than one, and indeed of several, orgasms at a time. Continue to explore your sensations after you have come and you may find that the next climax is better than the first.

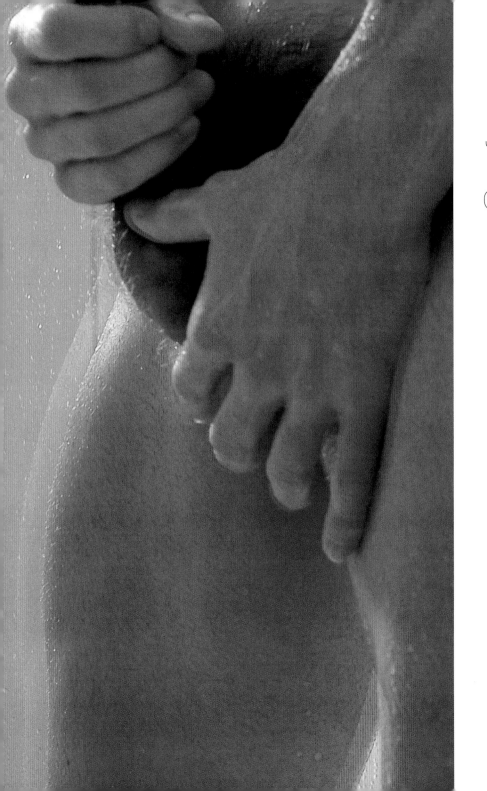

Satisfying Yourself

Men find that the same parts of their bodies are sensitive to arousal as women do – nipples, ears, neck, the inside of elbows and knees, inside the thighs, toes and fingers. As women react to having the labia caressed men respond to having the scrotum touched. Use your fingers and anything else that comes to hand to build up layers of sensation and reaction. Self-pleasuring can be all the more satisfying if you introduce different ways of fondling yourself – strokes, caresses, nips, pinches, scratches, even smacks.

Try directing water from a tap (faucet) or shower head onto the penis or scrotum. Pour some oil, or shower gel on to your skin and see how it feels to glide your hands all over your body, but be careful if you have any allergic or sensitivity reactions to soaps, shower gels or oils.

Use a feather, a silk scarf or a rough facecloth to tease, tweak and touch yourself. Try dipping a sponge first into hot water and then into cold before wiping it over the sensitive parts of your body. There is no point in rushing, so relish your enjoyment. If it makes you jump, pay special attention since pain and pleasure are often two sides of the same coin.

Bring yourself to full arousal and continue until you reach an orgasm. Remember this is not a race, take your time, and extend your pleasure before the climax.

Masturbation is good for you so make sure you are ready to let yourself enjoy it. Get relaxed, comfortable and create the right atmosphere, turn the lights down and turn the music on.

Men are sometimes more hurried in their masturbation than women, having learned when young to come as soon as possible to avoid being discovered. Rediscovering masturbation as an adult may be particularly helpful as it gives you the chance to retrain yourself to prolong your pleasure.

It is fastest and easiest to bring yourself to an orgasm just by stimulating your most sexually sensitive spot, but both your arousal and climax will be more exciting and satisfying if you arouse as much of your body as possible.

Start masturbating by touching your body all over. You may be surprised to find your mood has an effect on the way your body responds to touch. Linger over new sensations and see how far they will take you without losing your excitement. Bring yourself to a climax as slowly as possible and keep repeating your pleasure if you can.

Do not stop there. Both sexes find being hugged and held comforting after orgasm, so snuggle down and hug yourself. You are likely to enjoy the sensation of rhythmic stroking on your arms, face, and back for some time after orgasm.

TheJoysofMasturbation

Masturbation makes you feel good and makes you feel relaxed. Enjoying it does not mean there is anything wrong with your sex life and many women find it the most certain way to reach orgasm, eithr on their own or with a partner. Practising to reach an orgasm through masturbation makes it easier to reach climax during penetrative sex. Knowing how to stimulate yourself means that you can demonstrate exactly what moves your partner can make to turn you on.

Your clitoris is very delicate and sensitive and most women prefer not to start by stimulating their clitoris immediately. Try stimulating your whole body by touching and stroking yourself all over. Concentrate on the areas around your face, neck and ears. Move to your inside thighs, circling and brushing towards your genital area. Using a lubricant jelly can increase your pleasure as dryness in the genital area makes any stimulation, however gentle, painful and unrewarding.

Women masturbate in many different ways and each needs to find what works for them. You could try cupping your hand over your whole genital area, placing a finger either side of your clitoris, vibrating or gently stroking it. When you use your whole hand to cover and stimulate the area your fingers extend and direct the movements your hand is making so your fingers can focus on a particular area, increasing or decreasing pressure as you want.

Some women find the clitoris itself becomes ultra-sensitive and they prefer stimulation around the area, rather than touching the clitoris directly, while masturbating.

Some women like to use a finger in the vagina as they continue to stimulate their clitoris. They can move their finger in and out, or search for the sensitive area within or around their vagina. Many women prefer to carry stimulation right through their orgasm and many women find they enjoy following their first climax with further orgasms.

Following an orgasm, a woman's whole genital area is extremely sensitive and leaving your hands cupped in place without moving is as comforting as being held and hugged by a partner.

Masturbation definitely doesn't make you blind, deaf or insane. How often you masturbate is what is right for you. Use it, enjoy it and pass on what you learn about yourself to your partner.

Its easy to speed straight to orgasm, but you will miss out on the fun and the benefits on the way. For many men, masturbation is a very private activity they find difficult to talk about – so they don't. However, they may be missing out. Masturbation at the same time as your partner can advance your own pleasure and your understanding of how to please each other.

Start by arousing yourself all over. If music helps, turn it on or if you prefer the shower get ready. Stroke your body all over, lingering in areas you find especially stimulating, without, at first, touching your penis. Move your hands closer to your genitals, stroking your inner thighs and lower back, and enjoy the feelings rising within you.

Men have a variety of ways of touching their penis – many wrap the whole shaft in their hands, others touch only the upper surface, and others just the head of the penis. Their touch will vary from gentle strokin, to a firm grip. As ejaculation approaches, a man's movements become rapid. Some men prefer to cease any form of stimulation on ejaculation because the shaft of their penis becomes extremely sensitive.

During masturbation with their partner, many men find it exciting to tuck their penis between their partner's breasts, against her thighs or stomach. Lubricant can provide extra stimulation and protect the penis as well. Masturbation with a partner can provide a useful start to lovemaking, stimulating each other before moving to penetrative sex and orgasm. Make sure that you are in the right position for both of you to make full use of your hands, be patient and listen to your partner's responses to your touch and especially to what they are saying to you.

Masturbation does not mean anything good or bad about your sex life; in fact, men who masturbate and enjoy it are said to give and receive more pleasure from sex.

JoysOfMasturbation For Men

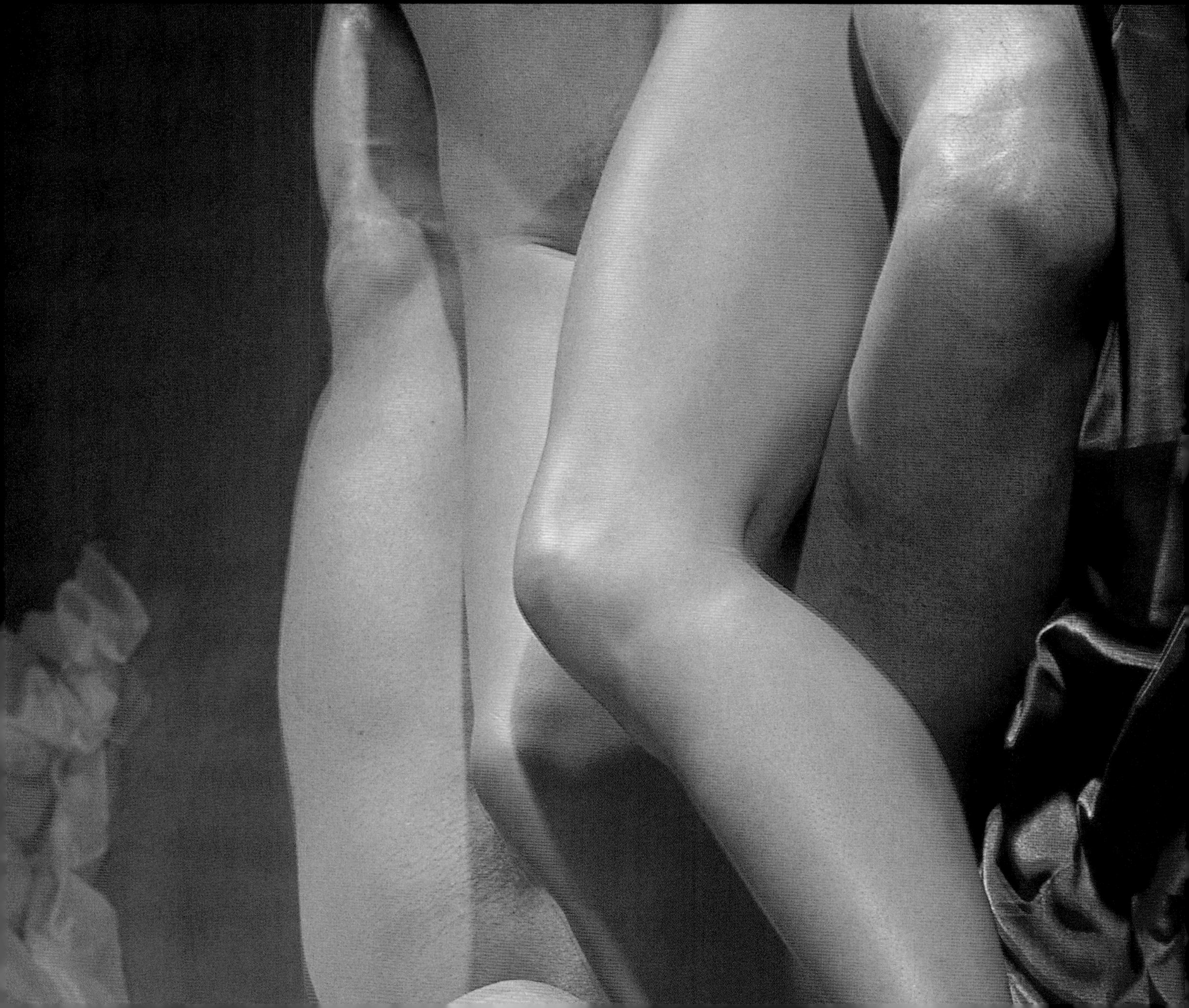

What can make lovemaking disappointing for many people is rushing straight to penetrative intercourse and orgasm. In trying too fast and hard you often cheat yourself of real pleasure. To bring fizz to your sex life, I recommend you try the technique called sensate focus. Sensate focus allows you to concentrate on the particular sensations you enjoy, bit by bit. Take time, slow down and enjoy the journey as much as the arrival. Enjoy or rediscover the fun of petting by exploring and caressing each other. The longer you take to build up to a climax, the more you enjoy the whole expansive experience.

Start by making a promise to each other that, for the time being, you will not have full sex. Instead, use your hands, fingers, lips, tongues, teeth, feathers, anything with which you can stroke and caress your partner's body. Increase your knowledge of each other, and to really develop your technique try 'no hands' sex. Not only is penetrative sex not allowed, you must not even use your hands or fingers to stimulate each other.

You can rub your bodies against each other and use tongues, lips, teeth, hair or toes in place of your hands. Try talking, whispering or blowing gently all over your partner. Take it in turns to bring each other to orgasm. Talk to your partner, and listen to them tell you exactly what drives them completely wild. You may both be surprised to learn what can bring either one of you to an orgasm, without penetration.

Don't forget being comfortable and warm is the best way to start. Many couples find music is still part of the language of love. Use your ingenuity and find out for yourselves that intercourse is one of the ways of pleasing each other, but not the only one. Touch and caress each other, starting with hands and moving up the arms to shoulders, around the neck and down the torso.

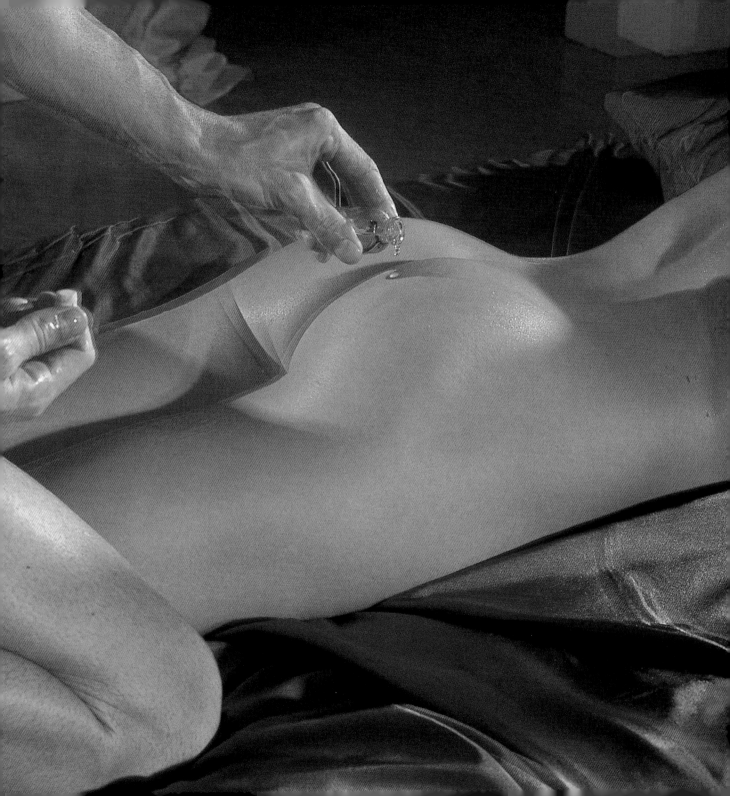

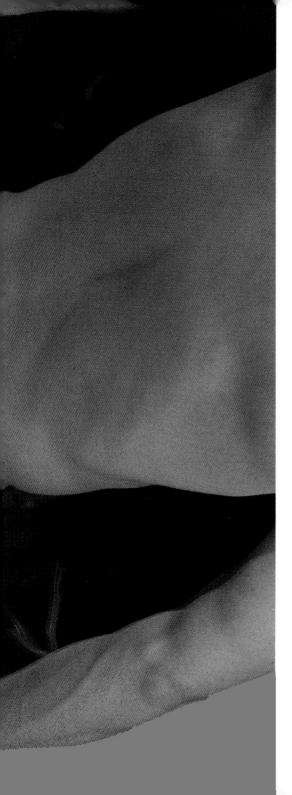

Turn and turn about, demonstrate to your partner what you have found in your sessions of self exploration. Touch your own body, and guide their hands while talking your partner through the how, where and why of the different caresses your body appreciates. Experiment! Use your nails to very gently scratch your partner, trailing your nails down their chest or back, or up their legs or arms. Only use pressure when and where they ask you to. Scratching can be very arousing but remember scratching can hurt too.

Prolong your sensual pleasure and enjoyment by leading slowly and inventively to a climax. You can bring your partner, and yourself, to a climax just by kissing. Very gently, nibble and nip around your partner's mouth and lips. Let the tip of your tongue stroke inside their mouth. Then probe deeper, caressing inside their cheeks. Thrust your tongue more firmly inside your partner's mouth and find out how aroused and satisfied you and your partner can be, simply with mouth-to-mouth contact.

Suggest to your partner that they lie face down, or sit with their back turned to you. Gently at first but getting stronger, rub, massage, stroke, need and scratch their shoulder blades, down the spine to the small of their back, their buttocks, and their shoulders. Cover the whole area and repeat your actions. The back can be a surprisingly arousing place when touched all over, especially around the neck and shoulders.

Using your thumbs, carefully knead and massage up the back of your partner's neck to the base of their skull. The shoulders and neck often carry tension which massage will release. Gently manipulate the area where their shoulders join their neck.

You can follow a massage by sitting face to face with your partner as close as possible, in each other's laps if it is comfortable. Caress your partner's face, from above the eyebrows, down the nose, up over the cheekbones and down the jawline to the chin. Extend the caresses down the chest, and stomach, to the genitals. Then take it in turns to tickle, tease, caress, nibble and kiss your partner's nipples.

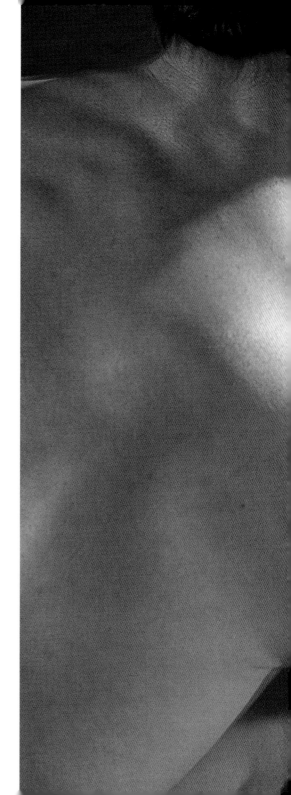

While sitting or lying face to face and close together, gently massage your partner's genitals. The outside of the labia or lips, if your partner is female, the scrotum if male. Slowly tease and caress the skin and then gently stroke down the inside of the groin and thigh on one side and back up on the other side. Keeping close to your partner so your bodies are touching, take one of your partner's feet in your hands. Kiss and caress it, taking special care of the toes. Sucking toes and licking in between them can be very arousing, to the point of climax. Most women can continue to make love after they have come to a climax, and many find it possible to have multiple orgasms. Men may be happy and able to go on caressing and pleasing their partners after they have reached an orgasm, but many find their interest subsides with their erections. Sensational sex sessions can come to a quick end if he reaches his orgasm too soon. Fortunately, there is an easy technique for a man to use to delay his climax. This is known as the 'squeeze technique' and it has two benefits. It means both of you can enjoy longer lovemaking and it enables a man to reach a bigger, better orgasm.

To use the squeeze technique, make love until the man feels he is about to come. As he feels the urge to climax, he tells his partner and withdraws, or you stop caressing each other. His partner takes his penis, spreading their fingers along the top of the shaft, close to his body. The flat of your thumb should rest just under the head of the penis, the glans, where the bridge of skin joins the bulbous head to the shaft. Press your thumb quite gently but firmly into the penis.

You need to be firm but not brutal; strong pressure will not hurt. The technique works if a man presses his own penis at this point, but it seems to work better if it is done by his partner. His urge to come will fade away. He will also go a little soft, but will keep his erection. Bring him back to full firmness and carry on. You can go on stimulating him until he reaches the same point, when you can repeat the squeeze – as many times as wanted, until the moment seems right.

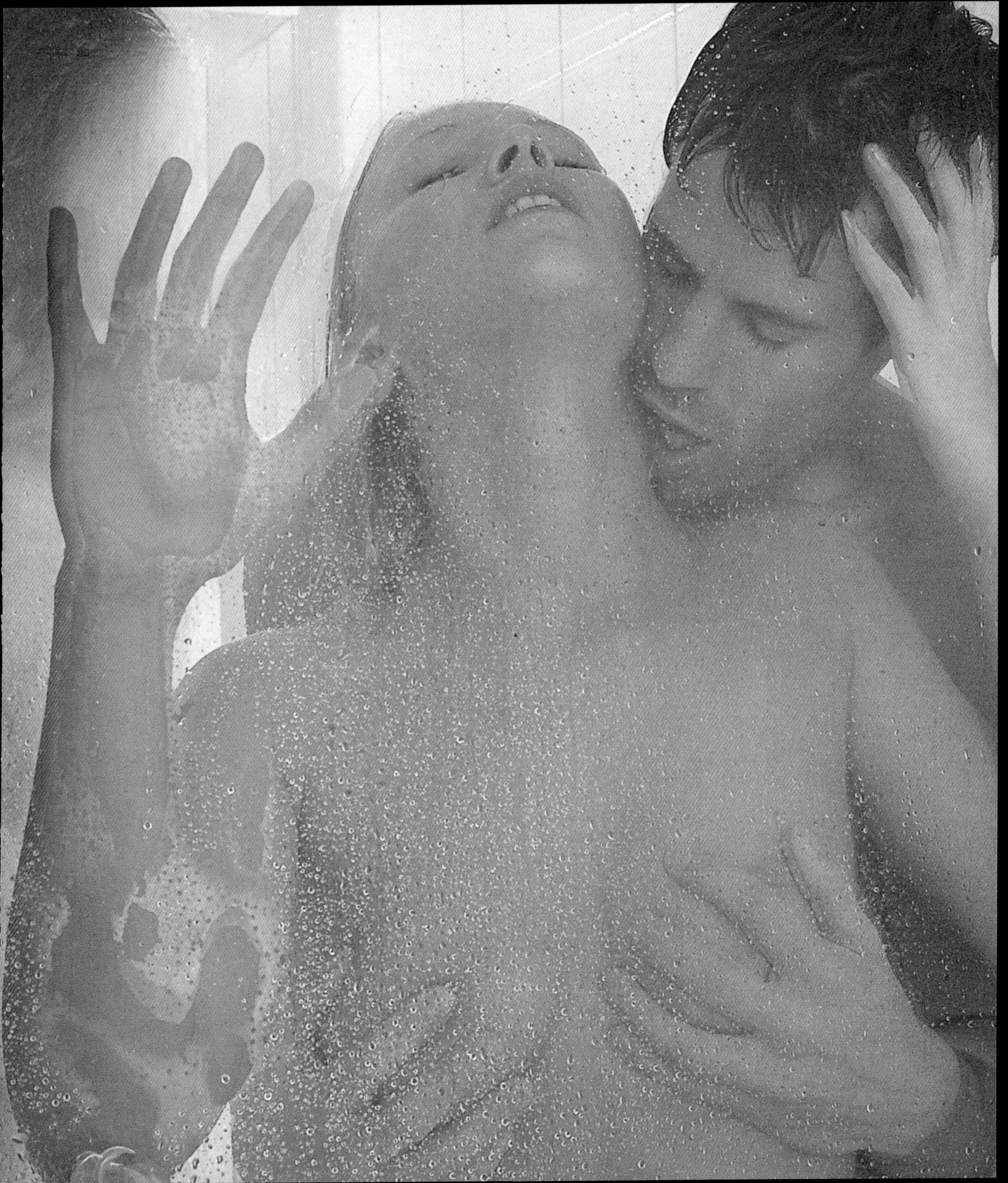

First Things First

Is there such a thing as someone who is 'good in bed' – a stud or studette? We all hear about bedroom athletes who are reputed to go on all night, arousing their partners to ecstasy, time after time. Is it enough ? There is the story of the Rolling Stones groupie who tried for years to sleep with Mick Jagger. She had sex with many other people and when asked how they were in bed always said, "He was good but he was no Mick Jagger!" She finally got her wish, and when quizzed said, "He was good but he was no Mick Jagger!" Apart from the fact that the fantasy may far exceed the reality, the point is that someone may know all the right moves but still not do it for you. Everyone is different and knowing how to turn yourself or a past partner on is no guarantee of knowing how to thrill your present bedmate.

The only way to be a genuinely good lover is to be sensitive and to ask your partner what pleases them. Try to act on what they are telling or showing you.

There is no "one size fits all" fantastic sexual technique, although knowing about the possibilities and variations available to you does make a difference. Always try to be considerate and open to suggestions. You can help your partner by being willing to talk about your own sexual desires. So how and where do you start?

If you want to be a good lover it helps to recognise what you have to learn. Instead of blaming yourself or your partner when things go wrong, be positive. Be the first to say you can do better and ask your partner to help you get it right.

Research shows that couples who talk freely to each other about sex are half as likely to have an affair as those who don't. Simply moving on to a new partner may seem to strike a spark first time but it won't improve your technique. Instead, take a leaf out of the book of people who stay happily together by sharing and caring. Talking about sex isn't about boasting about what you think you can do, but asking what your partner thinks and feels, and helping them understand your thoughts, sensations and feelings. The more you share your feelings, the better you will share your bodies.

When Marc and Casita asked for help with their relationship it became obvious that their upbringing had left both of them too embarrassed to talk about sexual matters. I suggested they buy some sex books and explicit magazines to look through. Not only did reading them together help them overcome their inhibitions and shyness but they found they could point to something that appealed to them and say, "Let's try that". Marc and Casita also acted on my suggestion to make a 'shopping list'.

The idea is for each of you to sit down and write down ten things you really want your partner to do for you, romantically or sexually. You can ask your partner to tell you they love you. You may ask them to say how good you're looking. Listing specific sexual favours you may say, "Please bring me to climax by stroking my nipples with a feather" or "I want to try oral sex with you tonight". As well as making a list of things you want your partner to do for you, write a list of things you would love to do for them. When you both have your lists, sit down together and share notes and agree to swap. Let each of you choose something you can do and something you can have done for you. Agree to give each other a treat, tonight.

As well as planning opportunities to please each other, be spontaneous. Relationships can go stale because it can all become predictable and routine. If you are suddenly overcome with the urge to grab your partner and have wild, passionate sex on the kitchen table instead of cooking the evening meal – do it! Don't hold back just because you have been together for some time and you think it is silly. If you are not alone, whisper in their ear that you have had this impulse and tell them you are only putting it off until a better time. Let the moment pass and you lose out on the sudden joy sex can bring. Have fun and make sex more than a regular habit!

Try new lovemaking positions as often as possible, they add extra spice to your love life. Exchange roles so each partner can decide in turn how, when and where you will make love. Some sexual positions – particularly women-on-top – are especially good for assisting female sexual pleasure; when he is entering from behind, both partners can use their fingers to caress her clitoris to make sure she is aroused and satisfied. Both these positions are far less tiring for a man so he benefits by keeping going longer.

SecondThingsSecond

LastThingsLast

Try a new place or time. Love lives can get stuck in a rut if you always know where and when – in bed, after lights out – you are going to make love. Set your clock an hour early and try an early morning kiss-and-cuddle, or go to bed early for an evening's fun. Try finding a new place: the kitchen table, living room floor, bathroom or stairs. Make sure you cannot be seen by your neighbours when choosing a different place. You will need to plan ahead so that you are both comfortable. Sharp edges, cold tiles can quickly turn an adventure into a sexual disaster.

Vary your pace. There are times when long, slow lovemaking is best. In the early days of your relationship, there might have been times when you were gasping for it and did not want to wait. Recapture the excitement by giving in to impulse and having the occasional quickie when you can.

Use your sexual fantasies to liven up your sex life. We all have them, and there is nothing wrong in indulging in a private reverie to give an extra edge to your lovemaking. Next time you make love, tell your partner what you would love to do to them in your fantasies; have sex on a deserted tropical beach, do a strip show, cover each other in chocolate and lick it off. Just describing it can bring back the spark between you. Adopt a role from your fantasy world and encourage your partner to enter your world by explaining who they are in your dreams. Speaking in character can be enough for many couples who are happy to talk to their partner. However, if you already have a fantasy you want to act out – such as dressing up as a member of the Police or Fire Service and doing a strip – agree to try it.

Fantasy is a part of most people's lives, a simple wish to be in famous person's place is a fantasy for most of us. You can start sharing your fantasy by saying if I was (this person) I would dress like this, live in this place where we could – the rest is your imagination. Fantasy is another way of just enjoying yourself and encouraging your partner to join in your dreams. It gives you a private world that exists only when the two of you are together.

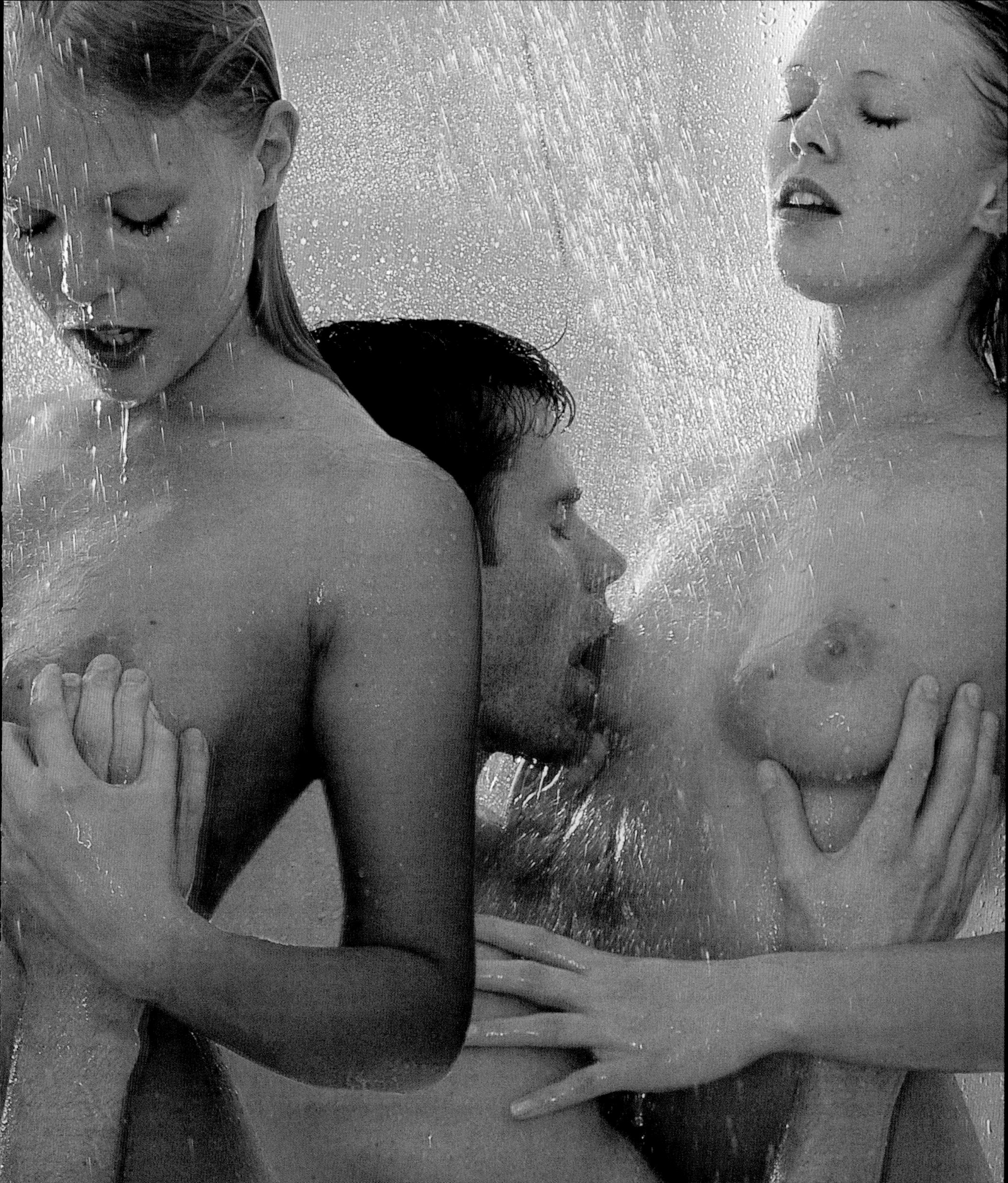

FemaleEjaculation

There has been a lot written about the G-Spot in the last few years, and we still are not sure that it exists at all. It is named the G-spot after gynaecologist Ernst Grafenberg who wrote about it in 1944. He said he had discovered an area in the wall of the vagina which, when stimulated, appeared to trigger not only powerful orgasms but a flow of liquid. He said this could only be described as female ejaculate. Men ejaculate when they orgasm and the two events are usually thought to always go together. Some men are able to train themselves to hold back their ejaculation, allowing themselves to experience several orgasms before reaching the end of their stamina. Grafenberg argued women could also ejaculate. Not all women are thought

to do so, and women who do ejaculate do not necessarily experience it each time they climax. However, a growing number of women do report that they produce varying amounts of fluid from the vagina when they reach orgasm. Some record feeling increased wetness after their climax, others say they produce a rush of liquid. Research into the theory shows that the fluid tested is neither urine nor simply vaginal fluid.

The prostate gland produces seminal fluid, which makes up 98 percentof male ejaculate. The suggestion is that some women have a vestigal (or small reduced) gland which is similar to the male gland. During sexual arousal, this vestigial gland swells and at orgasm can produce a gush of fluid. Although this has become and increasingly popular idea, many people are still not convinced that female ejaculation exists at all.

G-Spot

During sexual arousal, women who can find their G-Spot say that it swells up and becomes much larger, in a similar way to the swelling of the labia and clitoris and the walls of the vagina. The G-Spot is said to be especially sensitive when fingered and allows women to have particularly strong orgasms. To find the spot, gently insert a finger into the vagina and press the upper wall about 5 centimetres (2 inches) inside. You may feel a tiny pea-or coin-sized area slightly harder than the surrounding tissue.

Try finding it with your partner and discover how to excite the G-Spot with fingers or by using a sexual position such as rear entry, either while lying down, or standing up in the shower. Some women find it most effective for the area of the G-spot to be pressed, others to have that part rubbed. Together your aim is to make sure that the penis rubs against the upper wall of her vagina, to see if it produces specially intense sensations. Men can hold their penis as they enter, moving it around inside her vagina to allow contact to be directed to the right spot. Sex toys such as vibrators are also suggested as being good for finding and manipulating your G-Spot. Some have special shapes with a bend at the end to improve stimulation of the upper vaginal wall.

However, the fact that focusing on the top wall of the vagina produces pleasant sensations, enough to bring her to orgasm, does not necessarily prove that the G-Spot exists. The whole area around the vagina is a mass of sensitive nerves, and the clitoris and the nerves involved in clitoral stimulation lie along this wall. It is possible that pressing and caressing this area passes sensation to the clitoris and this is the reason that some women react so strongly to stimulation in this area.

The fluid that gushes out at orgasm could simply be vaginal lubrication, spurted out under the force of the strong vaginal contractions that occur during climax. Wherever the fluid is produced, there is nothing to be alarmed or surprised about if sex is a wet and squishy experience – that is exactly what it is supposed to be. If concentrating on this area does it for you, that's all that matters, and if it doesn't, move on and find out what does!

OrgasmAndErection

Men and women have many similarities in their physiology. Both experience orgasm and both have genitals that swell and stand out during sexual excitement. But there are also some particular differences.

A man's climax is delightfully and easily achieved by simply stimulating his penis, either by enfolding it in the snug, warm embrace of a vagina or a hand. This has led many people to assume that vaginal intercourse is also the best way for women to have a climax. If it works it for him, it should work as well for her.

For a woman to have an orgasm, however, she needs her clitoris to be stimulated and this is not always achieved by intercourse. It is true that the network of nerves connected to the clitoris sweep back an extraordinary long way from that small organ above and in front of the urethra or water passage. The clitoris has been estimated as having an area of sensitivity some thirty times larger, size for size, than a penis. This means that even during vaginal penetration movements in this area are transmitted to the clitoris, often leading to orgasm, but not always and for some women not at all.

Many women discover that they need either their clitoris directly touched by their own or their partner's fingers or to adopt sexual positions that allow the clitoris to be excited in other ways. Often, what makes a woman really enjoy sex is for there to be stimulation, direct and indirect, to the clitoris both before and after intercourse and for penetrative sex not to be the be-all and end-all of the act.

Taking your time in sex is an essential component for both men's and women's pleasure. This isn't about men being naturally faster than women to arouse or satisfy, as we'll explore in a moment. It's about both being able to approach love making at the same pace and at the same time. The more sex play you enjoy before you go for an orgasm, the bigger and better that orgasm will be, for both sexes.

MaleOrgasms

When men and women get aroused and go on to experience orgasm, they go through four distinct stages that are known as The Sexual Response Cycle. Both sexes experience very similar changes and feelings during this cycle and the cycle is the same each time you make love, unless you are interrupted.

The first stage in the Sexual Response Cycle is Arousal. This can be triggered by thinking about sex, or it can begin by someone touching you or making a sexual suggestion. During Arousal, men experience an erection of the penis and sometimes of the nipples. Time in Arousal varies. It can last as long as you want – a whole day or you can hurry through it in minutes.

The second phase of the cycle, Plateau, follows Arousal. Plateau is the heightened stage of excitement. It is the point at which you catch your breath because you know, any moment now, you are going to need it. Your face, chest, stomach, shoulders and arms flush a red or pink. Your penis and testicles increase in size; your blood pressure rises.

From Plateau you know, the third stage, Orgasm, is only thirty seconds to three minutes away. When the point of orgasmic inevitability is reached, you cannot stop it. During Orgasm, you pant and your heart pounds. Your body is overtaken by a series of muscular contractions that you cannot control. Ejaculation spurts out and your rectum pulses rhythmically for a few seconds. Following Orgasm is the fourth and final stage, Resolution. In reverse order the changes that happened during the first three phases return to normal. The flush recedes, the swelling declines and you breathe normally again.

Women, like men, go through the Sexual Response Cycle and, similarly to men, find their Arousal, the first phase, is triggered by thought, sight or touch. Most women experience some moisture in the vagina as a prelude to sex, which increases while they continue making love.

During the Plateau phase, breasts, nipples, clitoris and labia (the area round the vagina) swell and change colour. The pink sexual flush spreads across the face, breasts, stomach, shoulders and arms. This is why women wear blusher on their cheeks, to mimic the sexual flush and look attractive. During the Plateau phase, your blood pressure and breathing increase. Continued stimulation during the Plateau phase takes you to Orgasm.

At Orgasm, the third phase, your body goes through a series of muscular contractions. As well as pulsing in the rectum, the pulses can be felt in your vagina and womb. Following one orgasm, women can go on to have several more. Men go straight to Resolution, the fourth phase of the cycle when the body returns to normal.

Women also experience something called Carpopedal Spasm. This only happens when she reaches orgasm lying on her back when the Carpopedal Spasm can cause her toes to curl. It is possibly the origin of that Hollywood cliché when a woman who is kissed raises one foot by bending her knee in a kick of ecstasy!

FemaleOrgasms

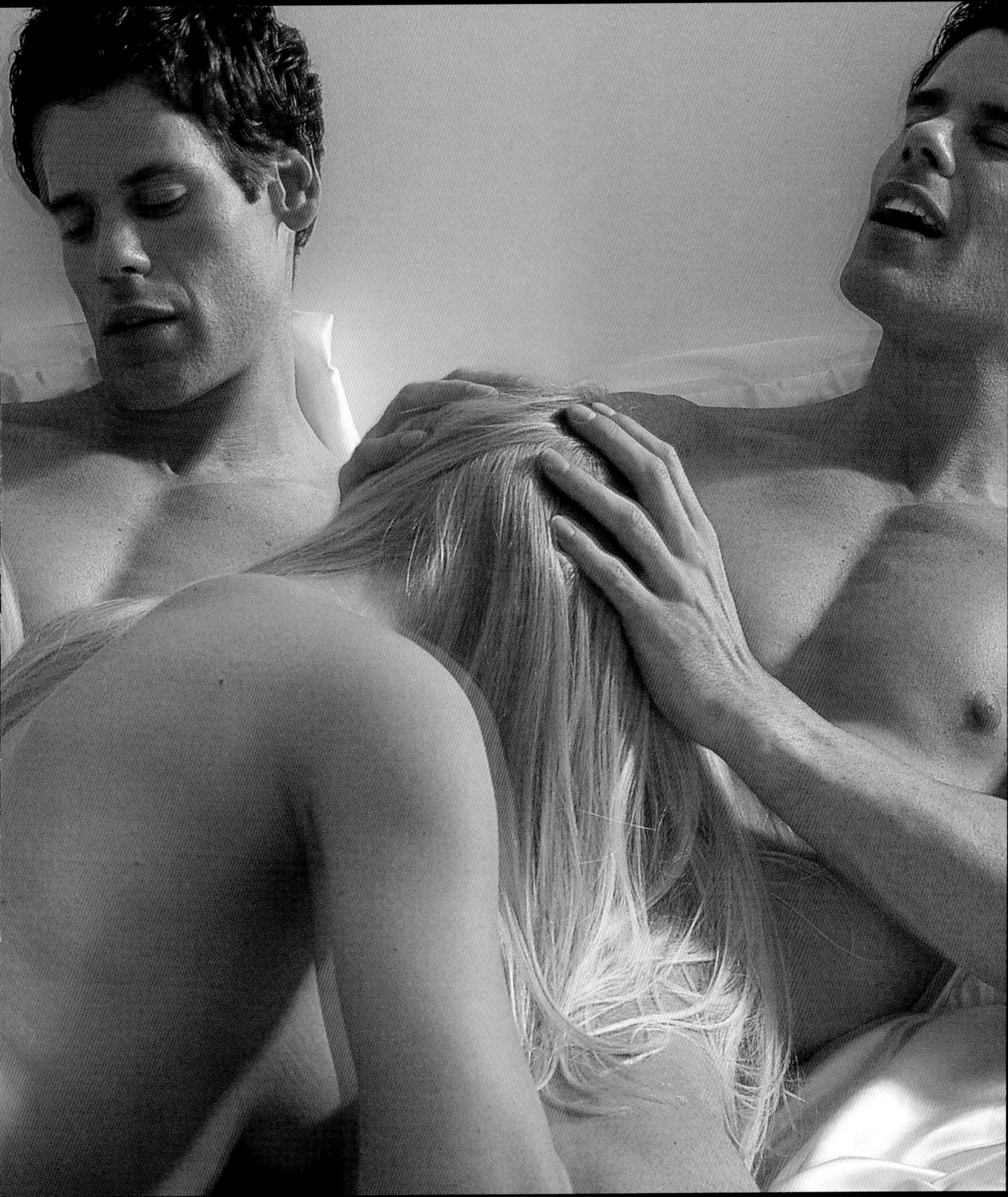

It's All Down To Timing

Timing for sensational sex depends on taking care of each other at every stage of the cycle. Partners should aim to leave the first stage of the cycle, Arousal, together so they travel together towards satisfaction. If one partner is very excited by the time a couple start making love, or if one partner moves too swiftly to orgasm, the other is often left dissatisfied. It is not that one of them is slow or frigid; it is because they started with a handicap and had no help in catching up. Timing depends on being sensitive to a partner's signals and communications. If you are both going to enjoy sex it is vital to let each other know what you are thinking, what you want and how, when and where to proceed. You are aiming to help both yourself and your partner, and to enjoy sex, either by matching your patterns, or by one of you lingering in Arousal, helping your partner to reach the same point before you both go on to Plateau and then Orgasm.

In the past, sex and climax were seen to be a male-only sport, with women playing a supporting role. "Good woman" were discouraged from showing any interest in sex. Later this attitude changed to an idealised model of sexual equality, in which the best sex was supposed to be found in simultaneous orgasm. It became a mantra. Couples climaxed together, or they fell short of the ideal and thought they had failed themselves and each other.

Now, it seems generally accepted that sexual enjoyment and satisfaction is whatever you want it to be. Some couples prefer to climax together. If this sounds right for you, you might like to pay attention to how each of you is feeling when you plan making love. So you both know what is on your minds, you might text, email or phone each other during the day. Alternatively you could leave each other notes, whisper sexy suggestions into each other's ears. This gives both of you the chance to anticipate the action and become aroused. When you get into action, pace each other. Have an eye to your own and your partner's excitement and help each other so you travel together. Other couples also find it fun, every now and then, to enjoy parallel orgasms. Instead of caressing each other, they masturbate together, watching and urging each other on to reach the same point at the same time.

When To Choose Your Moment

Consecutive orgasms are just as much fun. You can decide on who is to benefit first and then both put your energy and ingenuity into one partner's climax. With one partner sated and satisfied, you can together work towards an equally sensational climax for the other partner. Sexual excitement is usually stimulating for the partner who is witnessing the enjoyment. When both of you have had an orgasm that does not have to be the end. Either one of you may find capacity for more than one orgasm and many people enjoy slow, gentle and loving caresses more following a fantastic, fast, fabulous orgasm.

Resolution, the final phase, is inevitable, and although some people feel melancholy most find it a loving and supportive time. If it suits you talk to each other, whisper how excited you were by your love making. Enjoy the glow that good sex leaves behind, hold each other close and make plans for love making in the future. It is probably during Resolution that couples bond more closely in their partnership. The deep feelings of knowing each other are strengthened. You may fall asleep, a natural outcome of exertion and enjoyment, but make sure, before you do that you leave your lover feeling valued and loved, not ignored and abandoned.

Finding out about the Sexual Response Cycle gives you knowledge to help you both enjoy sex whenever you make love by watching for and pacing the stage your partner has reached. The four stages of the Cycle happen every time you get excited and go on to orgasm . Communication is important between you, at every phase of the Cycle, let each other know how its working for you.

There are no rules for achieving sexual satisfaction, which will be different for every couple and during the course of a relationship will change. However, use your knowledge lovingly, try not to start taking each other for granted or always leave the initiative to one partner. In a healthy relationship you should both be able to suggest, refuse and accept sex. Remember everyone needs praise and reassurance, fun and frivolity, and to be allowed to fail as well as succeed. You both need encouragement to explore and discover more about each other as the relationship develops and settles into and exciting and dependable partnership. Your enjoyment of sex should be able to continually change and flourish.

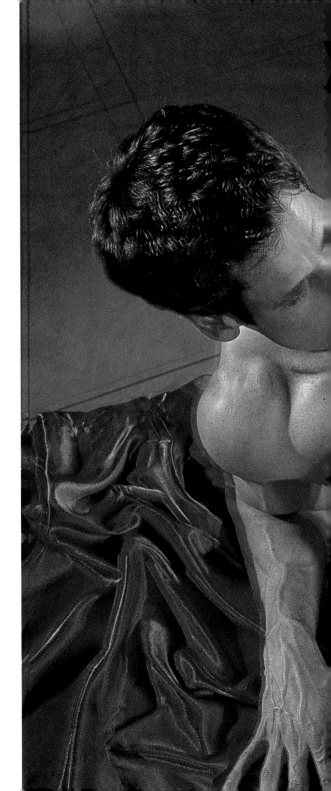

There is no such thing as the perfect ending. Just as there is no such thing as the perfect way to make love. The best ending happens when both of you are content. It happens when you are happy with yourself and your partner is satisfied too. It may not mean that you have both reached a simultaneous orgasm through penetrative sex this time or, indeed, that you have an orgasm, simultaneous or otherwise, by penetrative sex every time you make love. Sex can be mind blowing or it can be gentle and comfortable – either way can be what you want or need at the time. In other words the best ending fulfils your own expectations. It does not leave you feeling anxious about your performance, guilty that you have failed in some way as lover, embarrassed by your demands or inhibited and unable to communicate. Neither of you should feel you have let your lover down because either of you did not reach orgasm through penetrative sex.

Anxiety and tension are the biggest obstacles to feeling that you have arrived at a good ending. Trying too hard and seeing yourself as inadequate almost always lead to dissatisfaction before and after sex. Both men and women are vulnerable to feeling incapable or incompetent as lovers. When this happens, men might become demanding or critical, women might resort to faking orgasms. Your partner needs to know when they are pleasing you, and the sound of your sighs, moans, and murmers can urge them on. Even better, tell them in clear words when they are getting it right or show them how to please you.

If either of you feel let down and disappointed after making love choose how and when to tell you partner. This can be difficult when one of you drifts off to sleep oblivious of their partner's distress. Always focus on the positive, concentrating on what went right, to give them an incentive do what pleases you to make next time better. Praise them for pleasing you, and the chances are they'll repeat what worked. The best sexual skill for a good ending is learning how to communicate with each other.

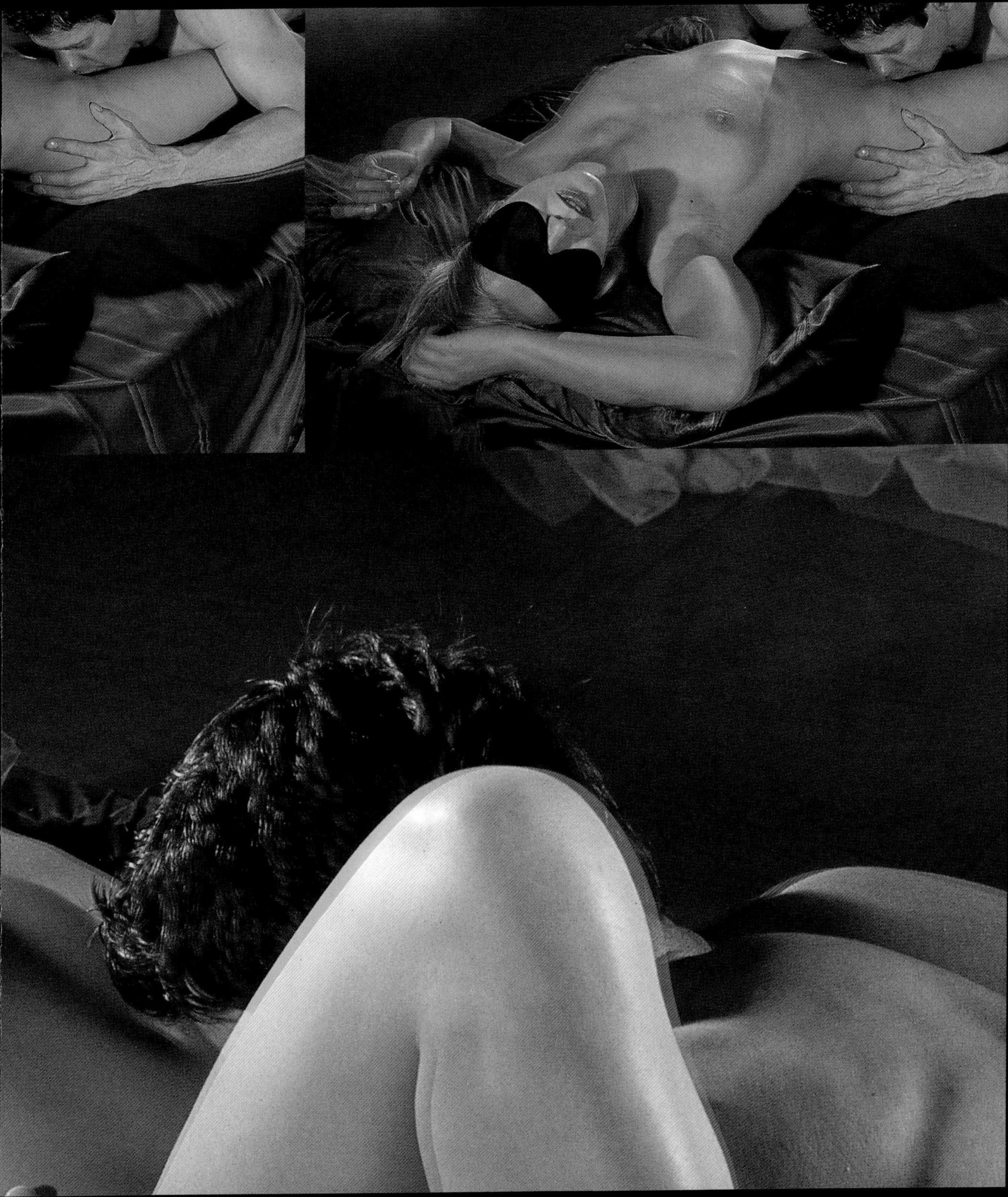

7 ▷ WhatTurnsYouOnAndHowToUseIt

You Only Have To Ask

We all have common erogenous zones, areas that are especially sensitive and sexually arousing. Breasts, nipples, genitals and lips are obvious ones, but ear lobes, fingers and toes, the soft skin inside elbows and knees, the small of the back and the nape of the neck can all be receptive. However, when it comes to what we like and dislike doing with or to them, or knowing how we like to make love, everyone is an individual. The only way you will know your partner's preferences is by being told or shown – communication is the key.

If you've been brought up with sex as a taboo, it's often hard to approach the subject without blushing or stammering. One way round is to use books or magazines and to point to things you'd like to try or talk about. You can always write each other notes or emails to say what you think you want to do but can't put into words.

We are not born knowing how to ride a bike or drive a car. To begin to do either we start by taking lessons and learning. However, when it comes to sex we expect ourselves and our partners to be experts, knowing exactly what pleases us and having an instinctive understanding of what might satisfy them. As an agony aunt I often receive letters from people complaining their partner does not seem to understand what would give them satisfaction. They feel their partner "ought to know what I need" or they are racked by guilt or a lack of confidence and say, "what's wrong with me, I should know what to do?" The truth is sex is the same as any other skill. To understand your own responses, as well as your lover's, you have to learn and practice.

Different people respond very differently when it comes to sex and sexual arousal. Some like gentle touches, others like heavier, rougher contact and one person may be turned on by something another finds unpleasant or uninteresting. None of us are mind-readers so the only way we can learn is by communication. Talking about what you like and dislike can have benefits. Most people would like some variety in their love life. They would like to try oral sex, or different sexual positions, but what holds them back is fear of rejection.

The more you talk to each other the easier it will be to talk about sex. Embarrassment tends to make us blurt things out bluntly or stops us saying what it is we want. An alternative is to point to some sexual option in a book or a magazine. The chances are that, far from being put off, your partner would also like some variety and will jump at the chance.

Try to avoid giving a running commentary or a barrage of instructions. You can make your needs known and understood with a wide range of non-verbal cues. Next time you make love, make a point of letting your partner know when they're hitting the right spot. Consider the following:

1. Be positive. Don't tell your partner you find them terrible in bed. Instead, think of something they did that you liked.

2. Thank your partner afterwards. When they light your fire, tell them so. It's called positive reinforcement.

3. Be honest. There is no point in faking excitement or saying you like something you don't, because that gives them no help to do better or to learn about you.

4. Do to them what you would like them to do to you. When they please you – demonstrate it by doing it to them!

Some times just talking about sex can in itself be exciting!

Get What You Want

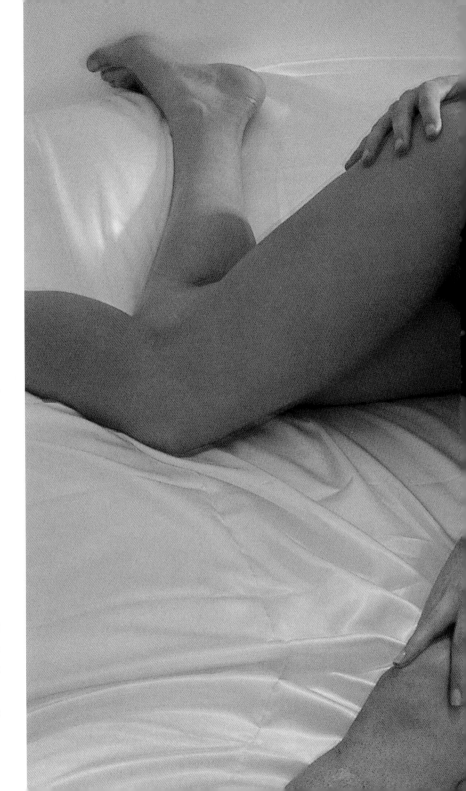

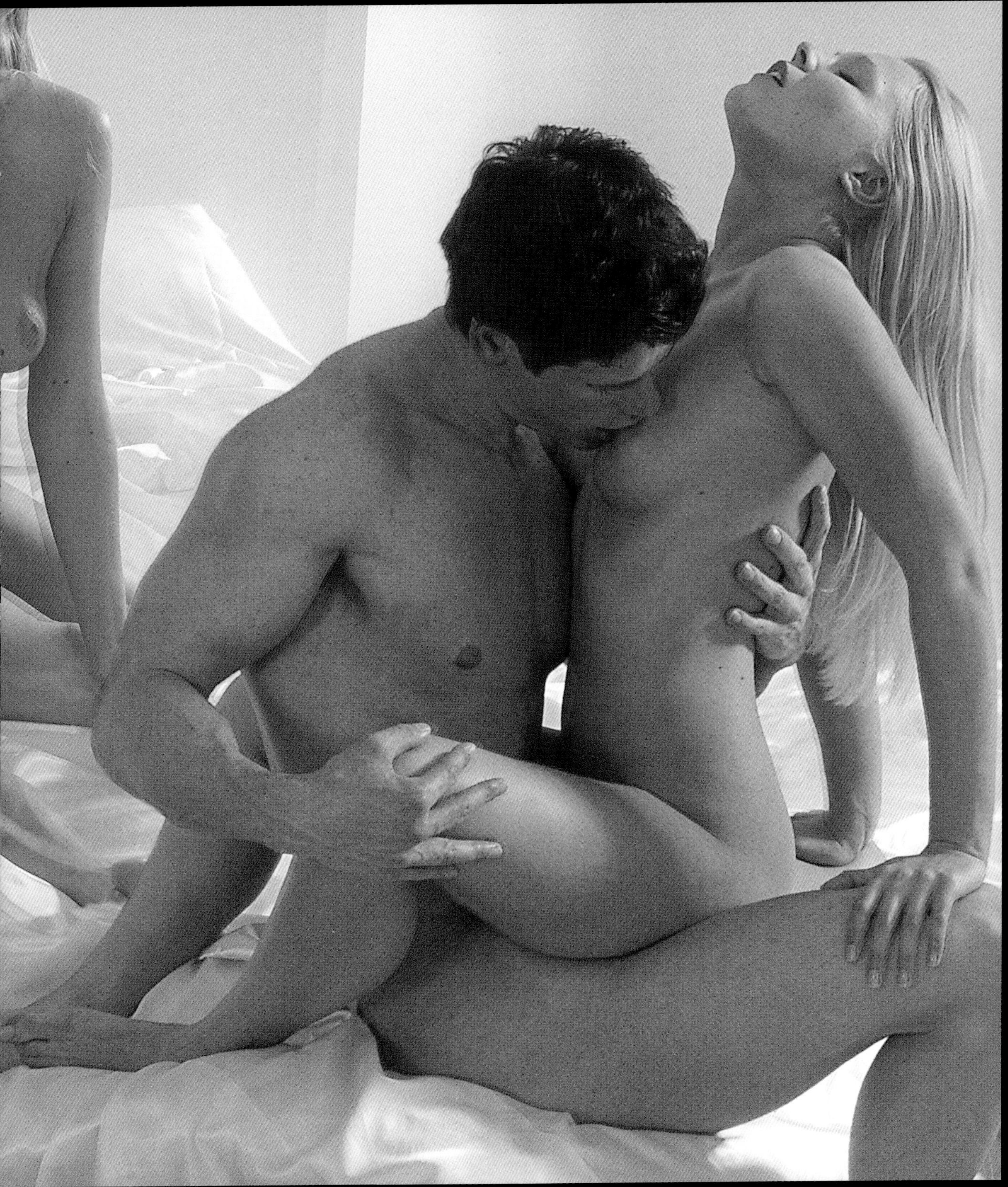

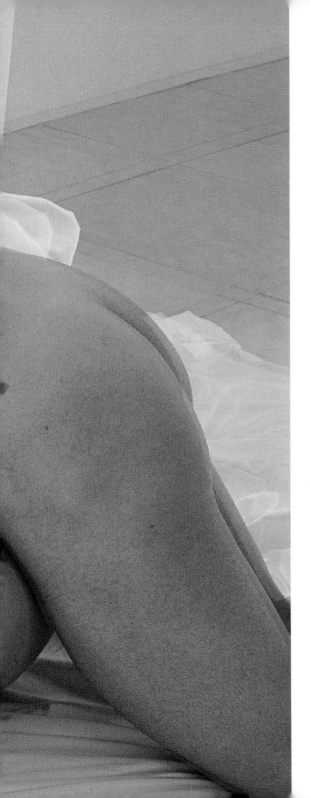

According to some sex manuals, there are over 500 different positions for making love. Advanced love-making positions do not guarantee ecstatic sex but they may help. You can use different positions simply for variety or to add excitement, or for a change of scene. Some are better for female sexual satisfaction, while others help men last longer. Some are more effective if you want to get pregnant, while others may feel naughty and wicked. Some are best for fast and furious sex, others for long, slow love-making. If you want to try a different position, try to ease your partner into it by gently rolling from one stance to a new one while you make love. The chances are that they will follow you like a dance partner and enjoy it as much as you. Be confident that trying new sexual positions is normal and can make your lovemaking even more fun.

Most people start their sexual life with the man lying on top. This position has several advantages for each partner. From this position a man can reach a woman's breasts and her clitoris, although to do this he must raise his body and support himself on one hand, while using his other hand to caress her. He can support more of his weight on both his elbows, allowing the woman to hold his buttocks or press down on the small of his back to steady and control the timing of his thrusts for her pleasure. The woman can raise her legs and wrap them around her partner's waist, or raising them higher, rest her shins and knees against his chest. A woman can bring her ankles over her partner's shoulders, a position that is good for deep penetration and is believed, for those couples intent on conception, to help this occur.

Lying side-by-side together is a position that provides long, lingering sex. The easiest position is to lie side-by-side with the woman's topmost leg bent at the knee and thrown over her partner's topmost leg. You can also lie thigh-to-thigh and one of you can hold his penis, and manipulate the end against her clitoris to provide lingering, mutual stimulation. Deeper penetration can be achieved if the man brings his knees up towards his chest and his partner lies inside his legs, her weight on his lower leg.

You can make love sitting up and facing each other. The man can stretch his legs out, so his partner can wrap her legs around his waist as she sits in his lap. In this position, you can hold each other close. Leaning back, you can caress each other's bodies and look into each other's eyes, caress and touch each other's face. You can also achieve this sitting on the edge of a bath, chair or bed.

You can make love face-to-face standing up, which makes for sensational bathroom sex-play in the shower. If you are the same height you can stand genitals to genitals, but if one partner is smaller and lighter than the other they can wrap their legs around the heavier and taller partner's thighs. The taller partner can hold them up for a short time by linking their hands under their lighter partner's bottom or thighs.

A position favoured by many women is when she is lying on top. Her partner then has his hands free to stroke her body, caress her breasts and nipples and to gently touch her clitoris. He can save his strength and last longer because he doesn't have to support himself. Women often prefer this position when, being in charge, they can control the speed, strength and angle of movement of his penis and find the point at

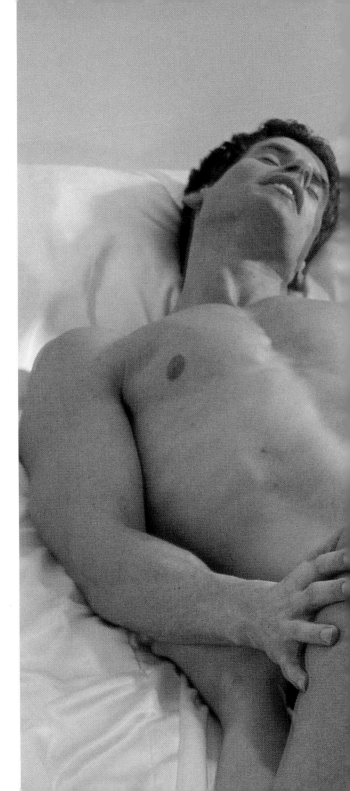

which the clitoris is best stimulated. Women usually find that if they ride quite high on their partner they are able to give themselves sensations that are particularly strong and satisfying.

There are a wide variety of woman-on-top positions. She can kneel or sit on his lap, leaning back using her arms to support herself. She can turn and sit the other way around on a bed or a chair . Sitting or lying, this is a position that gives the man the opportunity to hold and caress any part of a woman's body. It also gives him staying power and provides the woman with control and the chance to move and improve any stimulation which can considerably enhance both partners' pleasure.

Women-on-top

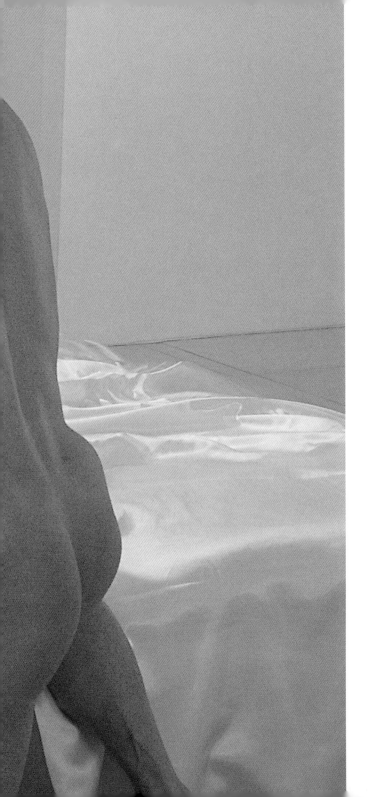

New Spoons

The rear-entry or doggy position has a wicked and animalistic buzz. You can come from behind in all sorts of ways, from standing up to lying down. In fact it is a very practical position because rear entry makes it particularly easy for either of the couple to reach and caress her clitoris and so bring her to a full orgasm. A favourite position is where the woman lies with her upper body propped up over pillows or cushions and her backside raised. He kneels between her legs and enters her. He can also stand between her legs as she leans over the side of a bed or chair. When a woman bends forward it makes it much easier for a man, holding on to his partner, to make deep thrusting movements. She can sit on his lap with her back either to him or turned halfway round, one arm around his neck, supporting herself slightly on her feet. This position limits her partner's movements so she is in control, raising and lowering herself to set the pace.

The last position for rear-entry sex is lying side by side, spoon-fashion. For lingering, unhurried love-making the spoon position provides maximum contact, skin-to-skin. The man can kiss his partner's neck and shoulders and has his hands free to touch and caress her all over.

The man may lie on his side with his thighs curled up and under her backside, her lower legs wrapped around his. Full penetration is easy in this position and by moving her legs to various angles, she can have a range of different sensations. Rear-entry sex is said to be the best position for stimulating the G-spot. With the woman lying on her stomach, legs apart and hips rotated slightly upwards, she can move her pelvis to make contact with the G-spot easy. Rear-entry sex can be achieved in a variety of positions: lying down, sitting up, or standing. It can be sensational, enjoyed in a bath or shower.

There are plenty of other sexual variations you might have heard about and like to try. Bondage, spanking, talking dirty - can all turn you on, or turn you off. Why would one person be excited by something another finds offensive, or downright boring? The reason is often found in the way we first learnt about and experienced sex. We often become fixed on elements associated with our early sexual arousal. A child who becomes aroused while being spanked may find, as an adult, corporal punishment excites them. If sex was a taboo subject in your childhood home, saying the words and talking dirty may be exciting for you.

If you have inhibitions about sex, you may also be drawn to bondage or punishment. Being tied up is a wonderful way of passing on responsibility for what is happening. If you encourage your partner to tie you up and have their way with you, you can console yourself with the thought that you are powerless to prevent what's happening. If a small voice from childhood always scolds you and disapproves of your sexual desires, you may find the only time you can relax and let go is when you can say to yourself that you are not in control. Using some sort of punishment such as spanking or being told to do chores can also relieve the guilt you feel about your sexual urges. Of course, being the one to tie someone else up or punish them may suit you as it can give you a feeling of power and control that you might not have had before in sex and love.

None of these, or any other variation, is unusual. Whether it is a problem for you depends on how you use it. If you cannot make love or be aroused without these additions and feel therefore you have problems then you may want to talk to a counsellor because being held hostage by your past is no help. But if it is just an extra when you choose to add it, the only question is whether you and your partner are equally happy to have this as part of your shared sex life. Discuss your ideas first, as surprise itself can be off-putting.

PositiveSex

Sock It To Him

Ask men what single sexual variation they would like to add to their lovemaking and most would vote for oral sex. This is the sexual act that produces the worst fears and apprehensions, yet would often give the most satisfaction. The very fact that it is still considered naughty, forbidden and even a bit dirty makes it exciting for some people. Being given oral sex by your partner can feel like the ultimate expression of acceptance. It can be the greatest compliment you can give your partner, to show them that you think they are good enough to eat. Many people fear their partners will find their genitals unpleasant to smell, taste or look at but you may find this is not what they feel. They may long to do it. If you would like to enjoy oral sex offer to treat your partner before asking them to try oral sex on you.

You can kiss, you can lick, you can suck or nibble around your partner's genitals. Some people prefer gentle movements, with their partner using lips and tongue to nudge them to arousal. Start off by gently running your tongue around your partners genitals to see how they react. You may then go on to firmer attention, tonguing and nibbling or even gently nipping them. Some people like having their clitoris or glans sucked, others prefer their partner to gently blow on skin first made damp by licking. Oral sex is commonly known as a 'blow job' but you should never blow into your partner's penis or vagina. It will not give either of you pleasure and may cause a potentially fatal embolism or infection. You can give each other oral pleasure – a man to a woman is called cunnilingus; a woman to a man is called fellatio – turn and turn about. Doing it together, at the same time, is known as '69' or 'soixante-neuf', from the shape your bodies make lying nose to tail. When one person does it to their partner, this is sometimes called a '68' – give it to me and I'll owe you one!

Sharing your sexual fantasies with your partner, may even involve dressing up and acting them out. It is important that both of you are in accord. There is nothing that kills a relationship as thoroughly and as easily as sexual bullying when one partner puts their own satisfaction above the other and sets out to get it by any method. It is always worth asking and discussing your sexual relationship because couples often harbour desires in secret that they would like to put into action and have only held back on from shyness and the fear that their partner would laugh or be disgusted.

There are a variety of ways you can tell your partner when you are interested in sex. You can also find ways of telling them how you want to go about it, without issuing a list of instructions.

Communication between partners is vital, and as your relationship continues make sure that understanding between you grows. The disadvantage when you think you know what your partner wants too well is that sex becomes a routine happening once a week. So imagine some new ways of sending your partner a message. Make it fun and enjoy yourselves. We have already looked at how body language – the way you stand or sit – sends messages about your thoughts and feelings. You could also try dressing-up or dressing-down. Meeting your partner at the door clad only in a thong is the most obvious of the dressing-down modes, but not the only one. Wearing clothes you know they like can be just as effective.

Make-up actually mimics the signs of sexual arousal – dark eyes, flushed cheeks and reddened lips. Take advantage of this by using make-up discreetly to get your partner going. Its especially effective if you don't normally use make-up, or use very little. You can experiment with blusher and lip colour in places that react to sexual arousal by changing colour. See what effect it has if you put colour on your ear lobes, nipples or inside your nostrils. There are some couples who shave or clip their pubic hair into shapes to make the point that this is something only the two of them see. Other couples prefer to shave off their pubic hair completely, leaving smooth skin.

A tattoo placed in an intimate spot such as below the bikini line, on the buttocks or shoulder blade can send a sexy message with a 'for your eyes only' flash. Piercings can add a spark to your sex life as well. You can have a stud or bar through your tongue, nipple, penis, clitoris, scrotum or labia. Genital and nipple piercings are not only for dramatic sexual display. Users say when they are tweaked or tugged they give exquisite sexual sensations and add to sexual arousal and satisfaction.

Playing Games Together

RulesOfTheGame

All of the sexual variations and ideas I have written about or are photographed here can make your sex life go with a swing. None of them are odd or unusual, and none are problematical in themselves. It is how you think about them that might give you problems. If you try to impose sexual experimentation on a partner who finds it scary or offensive, you are wrong and will not achieve what you are seeking. Either of you must be able to say No. It is not prudish or conventional to say "I don't want to do that!" Your partner should hear what you say and accept your point of view. An individual's idea of excitement does not give them the right or excuse to force it on another person.

If you are going to try bondage or spanking games, you do need to think and talk it through before hand. Some people get a real kick out of quite extreme treatment, and find smacking hard enough to raise marks may be thrilling and sexually arousing. But before you start you MUST have an agreed way of telling your partner if you want it to stop at once. Especially when part of the fun may be in screaming "Stop! Stop!" and your partner knows you don't mean it. You should agree a code word to use when you genuinely want it to stop. You also need to be sure your partner will respect the code. Never, never use bonds that cut off breathing or restrict blood flow. It can also be dangerous to bring other people into your sexual games, with an 'open marriage' or in a threesome. Like many others, you may well find the fantasy was fun but the reality is not when you find that one of the three has become more demanding or emotionally entangled than any of you expected.

Sex is a range of emotions and sensations. It does not stop with the first wild excitement of a love affair, it is not reserved for romantic moments and places, or for the young, slim and fit. A good, exciting, dynamic, and sensational sex life is for everyone, and everyone deserves it. The longer you stay together, the better it can be. Dynamic sex doesn't stop as you become more familiar with another person. You can often experiment with someone you know and trust, you are less shy with them. Open your mind, look around you and think what you could bring into your shared sex life. Make the changes and the additions, and talk to your partner. It really is simple, so go ahead and enjoy yourselves!

Sexually transmitted infections have risen over the last few years. People of both sexes, all ages and gender orientations find it difficult to negotiate safer sex, and some seem to believe that these practices are only relevant to HIV/AIDS risk and have little to do with them. But HIV/AIDS can affect everyone and anyone. What's more, while HIV/AIDS may appear to be the worst sexually transmitted infection you can contract, it's by no means the only one that can cause lasting effects. Hepatitis, herpes and genital warts cause both emotional and medical problems, and Chlamydia and Pelvic Inflammatory Disease can have a legacy of ill-health and infertility. What any lover needs to know is how to keep themselves and their partner safe, as well as the techniques to enjoy sensational sex,.

SaferSex

Safer sex practices may be seen as a code of behaviour about what you do during sexual activity to protect yourselves and your partners from all and any sexually transmitted infections. This can be helpful when negotiating sexual contact, and there is one, basic rule that should always be kept. This is: never share body fluids with someone about whose sexual history you CANNOT be sure. It's not enough to know the person – anyone can have a sexual infection, no matter how clean, nice or charming. So you should use a new condom every time you have sex, never have genital contact without putting one on first and be careful about risky practices that can cause scratches or grazes. If you have both always used safer sex practices, and are in a monogamous relationship, you can 'go bareback' together. But it only needs one person somewhere in your or your partner's sexual history to have had sex with someone who had been in contact with a condition

to pass it on to you. You can really only safely abandon barrier contraception if you have both been in a one-to-one relationship for over six months and have had a medical check-up at a sexual health clinic to see if both of you are sexually infection-free.

However, safer sex should be about far more than what we do in bed. It should also be about how we see, care for and value ourselves, and both our partner's and our relationship. We need now to focus on sexual health, and sexual health is about much more than HIV/AIDS and other sexually transmitted infections. Sexual health is a code of practice that covers all aspects of a sexual life. One of the best definitions is that of the British Family Planning Association which says sexual health is the capacity and freedom to enjoy and express sexuality without exploitation, oppression, physical or emotional harm. This definition recognises sexual health as a basic human right and celebrates the potential for sexual activity and sexual relationships of all kinds as being an important part of everyone's life. It recognises how our sexuality is a positive force for happiness, and that fun and pleasure contribute to our well-being. It also recognises responsibility to protect ourselves and our partners from all harm, whether physical or emotional.

With rights goes responsibility, with pleasure goes effort. We need not only to equip ourselves with the details of how not to contract and pass on sexually transmitted infections, how not to start a pregnancy unless a child has been planned and is wanted by both parents, but also to stop and think about the significance of our sexual behaviour to our own and our partner's physical and emotional well-being.